Roller Coaster I've Ridden: A Journal

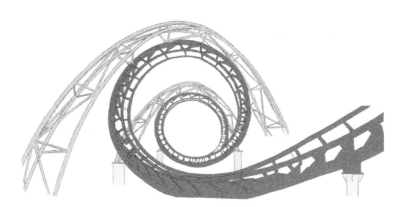

©2015 by Wandering Walks of Wonder Publishing

Printed in the United States of America

All rights reserved. No part of this work covered by the copyrights hereon may be reproduced or used in any form or by any means – graphic, electronic or mechanical – without the prior written permission of the publishers, except for reviewers who may quote brief passages. Any request for photocopying, recording, taping or storage on information retrieval systems of any part of this work shall be directed in writing to the publisher.

The Publisher: Wandering Walks of Wonder Publishing

Kansas City, MO 64118

USA

Website: www.wanderingwalksofwonder.com

ISBN-13: 978-1517375157

ISBN-10: 1517375150

This Journal Belongs to:

_____

The roller coaster is a popular amusement ride developed for amusement parks and modern theme parks. LaMarcus Adna Thompson patented the first coasters on January 20, 1885. Roller coasters are dated back to as far as the 16th century, in Russia. These were sleds going over ice covered wooded slides.

Roller coasters keep advancing as technology does. Roller coasters now spin as they go over the track, and others lay you down as you ride. These are just some of many types of roller coasters that have been created over the past years. From the first roller coasters to the ones today, roller coasters keep advancing as time does.

Types of Roller Coasters:

There are two major types of roller coasters, distinguished mainly by their track structure.

The tracks of wooden roller coasters are something like traditional railroad tracks. In most coasters, the car wheels have the same design as the wheels of a train -- the inner part of the wheel has a wide lip that keeps the car from rolling off the side of the track. The car also has another set of wheels (or sometimes just a safety bar) that runs underneath the track. This keeps the cars from flying up into the air.

Wooden coaster tracks are braced by wooden cross ties and diagonal support beams. The entire track structure rests on an intricate lattice of wooden or steel beams, just like the beam framework that supports a house or skyscraper.

They can even flip the train upside down (though this is rare in modern wooden coasters). But, because the track and support structure are so cumbersome, a wooden track is fairly inflexible. This makes it difficult to construct complex twists and turns. In wooden coasters, the exhilarating motion is mainly up and down.

The range of motion is greatly expanded in steel roller coasters. The world of roller coasters changed radically with the introduction of tubular steel tracks in the 1950s. As the name suggests, these tracks consist of a pair of long steel tubes. These tubes are supported by a sturdy, lightweight superstructure made out of slightly larger steel tubes or beams.

Tubular steel coaster wheels are typically made from polyurethane or nylon. In addition to the traditional wheels that sit right on top of the steel track, the cars have wheels that run along the bottom of the tube and wheels that run along the sides. This design keeps the car securely anchored to the track, which is absolutely essential when the train runs through the coaster's twists and turns.

The train cars in tubular steel coasters may rest on top of the track, like the wheels in a traditional wooden coaster, or they may attach to the track at the top of the car, like in a ski lift. In suspended coasters, the hanging trains swing from a pivoted joint, adding an additional side-to-side motion. In an inverted coaster, the hanging train is rigidly attached to the track, which gives the designer more precise control of how the cars move.

A tubular steel track is prefabricated in large, curved segments. The steel manufacturing process allows for a smoothly curving track that tilts the coaster train in all directions. A wooden roller coaster rattles as it rolls over the joints that connect the pieces of the wooden track. In a tubular steel coaster, the track pieces are perfectly welded together, making for an incredibly smooth ride. As any coaster enthusiast will tell you, each sensation has its own distinctive charm.

There are eight main coaster types:
- Sit-down: This is the more traditional type roller coaster where you are seated in a car. There are no special elements to this type of coaster.

- Stand-up: Similar to a sit-down coaster, this type of coaster you are standing up in the car instead of belted into a seat.

- Inverted: A roller coaster with trains suspended beneath the track above.

- Suspended: A roller coaster designed where the trains ride below the track rather than on top of the track.

- Pipeline: The track is attached to the middle of the train, instead of above or below it.

- Bobsled: Wheeled trains slide down a U-shaped tube instead of being fixed to a track.

- Flying: Riders start out in a seated position but are rotated to face the ground as the ride starts, giving the feeling of flying.

- Fourth Dimension: Two seats from each car are positioned on either side of the track. The seats spin or rotate on their own axis - either freely or in a controlled motion.

Date:	Name of Roller Coaster:	Track Type: ☐ Steel ☐ Wood
Weather:	Name of Park/Location:	Type of Coaster:
Year Opened:	Height:_____ Length:_____ Top Speed:_____	Designer of Coaster:

My Coaster Experience:

_____

_____

_____

_____

_____

_____

_____

_____

_____

Date:	Name of Roller Coaster:	Track Type: ☐ Steel ☐ Wood
Weather:	Name of Park/Location:	Type of Coaster:
Year Opened:	Height:_____ Length:_____ Top Speed:_____	Designer of Coaster:

My Coaster Experience:

_____
_____
_____
_____
_____
_____
_____
_____
_____
_____
_____

Date:	Name of Roller Coaster:	Track Type: ☐ Steel ☐ Wood
Weather:	Name of Park/Location:	Type of Coaster:
Year Opened:	Height:_____ Length:_____ Top Speed:_____	Designer of Coaster:

My Coaster Experience:

_____
_____
_____
_____
_____
_____
_____
_____
_____
_____
_____

Date:	Name of Roller Coaster:	Track Type: ☐ Steel ☐ Wood
Weather: ☀ ⛅ 🌧 🌨	Name of Park/Location:	Type of Coaster:
Year Opened:	Height:_____ Length:_____ Top Speed:_____	Designer of Coaster:

My Coaster Experience:

_____

_____

_____

_____

_____

_____

_____

_____

_____

Date:	Name of Roller Coaster:	Track Type: ☐ Steel ☐ Wood
Weather:	Name of Park/Location:	Type of Coaster:
Year Opened:	Height:_____ Length:_____ Top Speed:_____	Designer of Coaster:

My Coaster Experience:

_____

_____

_____

_____

_____

_____

_____

_____

_____

Date:	Name of Roller Coaster:	Track Type: ☐ Steel ☐ Wood
Weather: ☀ ⛅ 🌧 🌨	Name of Park/Location:	Type of Coaster:
Year Opened:	Height:_____ Length:_____ Top Speed:_____	Designer of Coaster:

My Coaster Experience:

_____
_____
_____
_____
_____
_____
_____
_____
_____
_____
_____

Date:	Name of Roller Coaster:	Track Type: ☐ Steel ☐ Wood
Weather:	Name of Park/Location:	Type of Coaster:
Year Opened:	Height:_____ Length:_____ Top Speed:_____	Designer of Coaster:

My Coaster Experience:

_____
_____
_____
_____
_____
_____
_____
_____
_____
_____
_____
_____

Date:	Name of Roller Coaster:	Track Type: ☐ Steel ☐ Wood
Weather:	Name of Park/Location:	Type of Coaster:
Year Opened:	Height:_____ Length:_____ Top Speed:_____	Designer of Coaster:

My Coaster Experience:

_____
_____
_____
_____
_____
_____
_____
_____
_____
_____

Date:	Name of Roller Coaster:	Track Type: ☐ Steel ☐ Wood
Weather:	Name of Park/Location:	Type of Coaster:
Year Opened:	Height:_____ Length:_____ Top Speed:_____	Designer of Coaster:

My Coaster Experience:

_____
_____
_____
_____
_____
_____
_____
_____
_____
_____

Date:	Name of Roller Coaster:	Track Type: ☐ Steel ☐ Wood
Weather:	Name of Park/Location:	Type of Coaster:
Year Opened:	Height:_____ Length:_____ Top Speed:_____	Designer of Coaster:

My Coaster Experience:

_____
_____
_____
_____
_____
_____
_____
_____
_____
_____

Date:	Name of Roller Coaster:	Track Type: ☐ Steel ☐ Wood
Weather: ☼ ⛅ 🌧 🌨	Name of Park/Location:	Type of Coaster:
Year Opened	Height:_____ Length:_____ Top Speed:_____	Designer of Coaster:

My Coaster Experience:

_____
_____
_____
_____
_____
_____
_____
_____
_____
_____

Date:	Name of Roller Coaster:	Track Type: ☐ Steel ☐ Wood
Weather: ☀ ⛅ 🌧 ☁	Name of Park/Location:	Type of Coaster:
Year Opened:	Height:_____ Length:_____ Top Speed:_____	Designer of Coaster:

My Coaster Experience:

_____
_____
_____
_____
_____
_____
_____
_____
_____
_____
_____

Date:	Name of Roller Coaster:	Track Type: ☐ Steel ☐ Wood
Weather:	Name of Park/Location:	Type of Coaster:
Year Opened:	Height:_____ Length:_____ Top Speed:_____	Designer of Coaster:

My Coaster Experience:

_____

_____

_____

_____

_____

_____

_____

_____

_____

_____

Date:	Name of Roller Coaster:	Track Type: ☐ Steel ☐ Wood
Weather: ☀ ⛅ 🌧 🌨	Name of Park/Location:	Type of Coaster:
Year Opened:	Height:_____ Length:_____ Top Speed:_____	Designer of Coaster:

My Coaster Experience:

_____

_____

_____

_____

_____

_____

_____

_____

_____

_____

Date:	Name of Roller Coaster:	Track Type: ☐ Steel ☐ Wood
Weather: ☀ ⛅ 🌧 🌨	Name of Park/Location:	Type of Coaster:
Year Opened:	Height:_____ Length:_____ Top Speed:_____	Designer of Coaster:

My Coaster Experience:

_____
_____
_____
_____
_____
_____
_____
_____
_____
_____
_____

Date:	Name of Roller Coaster:	Track Type: ☐ Steel ☐ Wood
Weather:	Name of Park/Location:	Type of Coaster:
Year Opened:	Height:_____ Length:_____ Top Speed:_____	Designer of Coaster:

My Coaster Experience:

_____
_____
_____
_____
_____
_____
_____
_____
_____
_____

Date:	Name of Roller Coaster:	Track Type: ☐ Steel ☐ Wood
Weather:	Name of Park/Location:	Type of Coaster:
Year Opened:	Height:_____ Length:_____ Top Speed:_____	Designer of Coaster:

My Coaster Experience:

_____
_____
_____
_____
_____
_____
_____
_____
_____
_____

Date:	Name of Roller Coaster:	Track Type: ☐ Steel ☐ Wood
Weather:	Name of Park/Location:	Type of Coaster:
Year Opened:	Height:_____ Length:_____ Top Speed:_____	Designer of Coaster:

My Coaster Experience:

_____

_____

_____

_____

_____

_____

_____

_____

_____

_____

Date:	Name of Roller Coaster:	Track Type: ☐ Steel ☐ Wood
Weather:	Name of Park/Location:	Type of Coaster:
Year Opened:	Height:_____ Length:_____ Top Speed:_____	Designer of Coaster:

My Coaster Experience:

_____

_____

_____

_____

_____

_____

_____

_____

_____

_____

Date:	Name of Roller Coaster:	Track Type: ☐ Steel ☐ Wood
Weather:	Name of Park/Location:	Type of Coaster:
Year Opened:	Height:_____ Length:_____ Top Speed:_____	Designer of Coaster:

My Coaster Experience:

_____

_____

_____

_____

_____

_____

_____

_____

_____

_____

_____

Date:	Name of Roller Coaster:	Track Type: ☐ Steel ☐ Wood
Weather:	Name of Park/Location:	Type of Coaster:
Year Opened:	Height:_____ Length:_____ Top Speed:_____	Designer of Coaster:

My Coaster Experience:

_____
_____
_____
_____
_____
_____
_____
_____
_____
_____
_____

Date:	Name of Roller Coaster:	Track Type: ☐ Steel ☐ Wood
Weather:	Name of Park/Location:	Type of Coaster:
Year Opened:	Height:_____ Length:_____ Top Speed:_____	Designer of Coaster:

My Coaster Experience:

_____

_____

_____

_____

_____

_____

_____

_____

_____

_____

Date:	Name of Roller Coaster:	Track Type: ☐ Steel ☐ Wood
Weather:	Name of Park/Location:	Type of Coaster:
Year Opened:	Height:_____ Length:_____ Top Speed:_____	Designer of Coaster:

My Coaster Experience:

_____

_____

_____

_____

_____

_____

_____

_____

_____

_____

Date:	Name of Roller Coaster:	Track Type: ☐ Steel ☐ Wood
Weather:	Name of Park/Location:	Type of Coaster:
Year Opened:	Height:_____ Length:_____ Top Speed:_____	Designer of Coaster:

My Coaster Experience:

_____
_____
_____
_____
_____
_____
_____
_____
_____
_____
_____

Date:	Name of Roller Coaster:	Track Type: ☐ Steel ☐ Wood
Weather:	Name of Park/Location:	Type of Coaster:
Year Opened:	Height:_____ Length:_____ Top Speed:_____	Designer of Coaster:

My Coaster Experience:

_____
_____
_____
_____
_____
_____
_____
_____
_____
_____
_____

Date:	Name of Roller Coaster:	Track Type: ☐ Steel ☐ Wood
Weather: ☀ ⛅ 🌧 🌨	Name of Park/Location:	Type of Coaster:
Year Opened:	Height:_____ Length:_____ Top Speed:_____	Designer of Coaster:

My Coaster Experience:

_____
_____
_____
_____
_____
_____
_____
_____
_____
_____
_____

Date:	Name of Roller Coaster:	Track Type: ☐ Steel ☐ Wood
Weather:	Name of Park/Location:	Type of Coaster:
Year Opened:	Height:_____ Length:_____ Top Speed:_____	Designer of Coaster:

My Coaster Experience:

_____
_____
_____
_____
_____
_____
_____
_____
_____
_____
_____

Date:	Name of Roller Coaster:	Track Type: ☐ Steel ☐ Wood
Weather:	Name of Park/Location:	Type of Coaster:
Year Opened:	Height:_____ Length:_____ Top Speed:_____	Designer of Coaster:

My Coaster Experience:
_____
_____
_____
_____
_____
_____
_____
_____
_____
_____

Date:	Name of Roller Coaster:	Track Type: ☐ Steel ☐ Wood
Weather: ☀ ⛅ 🌧 🌨	Name of Park/Location:	Type of Coaster:
Year Opened:	Height:_____ Length:_____ Top Speed:_____	Designer of Coaster:

My Coaster Experience:

_____
_____
_____
_____
_____
_____
_____
_____
_____
_____

Date:	Name of Roller Coaster:	Track Type: ☐ Steel ☐ Wood
Weather: ☀ ⛅ 🌧 🌨	Name of Park/Location:	Type of Coaster:
Year Opened:	Height:_____ Length:_____ Top Speed:_____	Designer of Coaster:

My Coaster Experience:

_____
_____
_____
_____
_____
_____
_____
_____
_____
_____

Date:	Name of Roller Coaster:	Track Type: ☐ Steel ☐ Wood
Weather:	Name of Park/Location:	Type of Coaster:
Year Opened:	Height:_____ Length:_____ Top Speed:_____	Designer of Coaster:

My Coaster Experience:

_____
_____
_____
_____
_____
_____
_____
_____
_____
_____

Date:	Name of Roller Coaster:	Track Type: ☐ Steel ☐ Wood
Weather:	Name of Park/Location:	Type of Coaster:
Year Opened:	Height:_____ Length:_____ Top Speed:_____	Designer of Coaster:

My Coaster Experience:

_____
_____
_____
_____
_____
_____
_____
_____
_____

Date:	Name of Roller Coaster:	Track Type: ☐ Steel ☐ Wood
Weather:	Name of Park/Location:	Type of Coaster:
Year Opened:	Height:_____ Length:_____ Top Speed:_____	Designer of Coaster:

My Coaster Experience:

_____

_____

_____

_____

_____

_____

_____

_____

_____

_____

Date:	Name of Roller Coaster:	Track Type: ☐ Steel ☐ Wood
Weather: ☀ ⛅ 🌧 ☁	Name of Park/Location:	Type of Coaster:
Year Opened:	Height:_____ Length:_____ Top Speed:_____	Designer of Coaster:

My Coaster Experience:

_____
_____
_____
_____
_____
_____
_____
_____
_____
_____

Date:	Name of Roller Coaster:	Track Type: ☐ Steel ☐ Wood
Weather:	Name of Park/Location:	Type of Coaster:
Year Opened:	Height:_____ Length:_____ Top Speed:_____	Designer of Coaster:

My Coaster Experience:

_____
_____
_____
_____
_____
_____
_____
_____
_____
_____

Date:	Name of Roller Coaster:	Track Type: ☐ Steel ☐ Wood
Weather:	Name of Park/Location:	Type of Coaster:
Year Opened:	Height:_____ Length:_____ Top Speed:_____	Designer of Coaster:

My Coaster Experience:

_____
_____
_____
_____
_____
_____
_____
_____
_____
_____
_____

Date:	Name of Roller Coaster:	Track Type: ☐ Steel ☐ Wood
Weather:	Name of Park/Location:	Type of Coaster:
Year Opened:	Height:_____ Length:_____ Top Speed:_____	Designer of Coaster:

My Coaster Experience:

_____
_____
_____
_____
_____
_____
_____
_____
_____
_____
_____

Date:	Name of Roller Coaster:	Track Type: ☐ Steel ☐ Wood
Weather: ☀ ⛅ 🌧 🌨	Name of Park/Location:	Type of Coaster:
Year Opened:	Height:_____ Length:_____ Top Speed:_____	Designer of Coaster:

My Coaster Experience:

_____
_____
_____
_____
_____
_____
_____
_____
_____
_____

Date:	Name of Roller Coaster:	Track Type: ☐ Steel ☐ Wood
Weather:	Name of Park/Location:	Type of Coaster:
Year Opened:	Height:_____ Length:_____ Top Speed:_____	Designer of Coaster:

My Coaster Experience:

_____

_____

_____

_____

_____

_____

_____

_____

_____

_____

Date:	Name of Roller Coaster:	Track Type: ☐ Steel ☐ Wood
Weather:	Name of Park/Location:	Type of Coaster:
Year Opened:	Height:_____ Length:_____ Top Speed:_____	Designer of Coaster:

My Coaster Experience:

_____
_____
_____
_____
_____
_____
_____
_____
_____

Date:	Name of Roller Coaster:	Track Type: ☐ Steel ☐ Wood
Weather:	Name of Park/Location:	Type of Coaster:
Year Opened:	Height:_____ Length:_____ Top Speed:_____	Designer of Coaster:

My Coaster Experience:

_____
_____
_____
_____
_____
_____
_____
_____
_____
_____

Date:	Name of Roller Coaster:	Track Type: ☐ Steel ☐ Wood
Weather:	Name of Park/Location:	Type of Coaster:
Year Opened:	Height:_____ Length:_____ Top Speed:_____	Designer of Coaster:

My Coaster Experience:

_____
_____
_____
_____
_____
_____
_____
_____
_____
_____

Date:	Name of Roller Coaster:	Track Type: ☐ Steel ☐ Wood
Weather:	Name of Park/Location:	Type of Coaster:
Year Opened:	Height:_____ Length:_____ Top Speed:_____	Designer of Coaster:

My Coaster Experience:

_____

_____

_____

_____

_____

_____

_____

_____

_____

_____

_____

Date:	Name of Roller Coaster:	Track Type: ☐ Steel ☐ Wood
Weather:	Name of Park/Location:	Type of Coaster:
Year Opened:	Height: _____ Length: _____ Top Speed: _____	Designer of Coaster:

My Coaster Experience:

_____
_____
_____
_____
_____
_____
_____
_____
_____
_____

Date:	Name of Roller Coaster:	Track Type: ☐ Steel ☐ Wood
Weather:	Name of Park/Location:	Type of Coaster:
Year Opened:	Height:_____ Length:_____ Top Speed:_____	Designer of Coaster:

My Coaster Experience:

_____

_____

_____

_____

_____

_____

_____

_____

_____

_____

Date:	Name of Roller Coaster:	Track Type: ☐ Steel ☐ Wood
Weather: ☀ ⛅ 🌧 ❄	Name of Park/Location:	Type of Coaster:
Year Opened:	Height:_____ Length:_____ Top Speed:_____	Designer of Coaster:

My Coaster Experience:

_____
_____
_____
_____
_____
_____
_____
_____
_____
_____

Date:	Name of Roller Coaster:	Track Type: ☐ Steel ☐ Wood
Weather:	Name of Park/Location:	Type of Coaster:
Year Opened:	Height:_____ Length:_____ Top Speed:_____	Designer of Coaster:

My Coaster Experience: _____
_____
_____
_____
_____
_____
_____
_____
_____
_____
_____

Date:	Name of Roller Coaster:	Track Type: ☐ Steel ☐ Wood
Weather:	Name of Park/Location:	Type of Coaster:
Year Opened:	Height:_____ Length:_____ Top Speed:_____	Designer of Coaster:

My Coaster Experience:

_____
_____
_____
_____
_____
_____
_____
_____
_____
_____

Date:	Name of Roller Coaster:	Track Type: ☐ Steel ☐ Wood
Weather:	Name of Park/Location:	Type of Coaster:
Year Opened:	Height:_____ Length:_____ Top Speed:_____	Designer of Coaster:

My Coaster Experience:

_____
_____
_____
_____
_____
_____
_____
_____
_____
_____

Date:	Name of Roller Coaster:	Track Type: ☐ Steel ☐ Wood
Weather:	Name of Park/Location:	Type of Coaster:
Year Opened:	Height:_____ Length:_____ Top Speed:_____	Designer of Coaster:

My Coaster Experience:
_____
_____
_____
_____
_____
_____
_____
_____
_____
_____
_____

Date:	Name of Roller Coaster:	Track Type: ☐ Steel ☐ Wood
Weather:	Name of Park/Location:	Type of Coaster:
Year Opened:	Height:_____ Length:_____ Top Speed:_____	Designer of Coaster:

My Coaster Experience:

_____

_____

_____

_____

_____

_____

_____

_____

_____

_____

Date:	Name of Roller Coaster:	Track Type: ☐ Steel ☐ Wood
Weather:	Name of Park/Location:	Type of Coaster:
Year Opened:	Height:_____ Length:_____ Top Speed:_____	Designer of Coaster:

My Coaster Experience:

_____
_____
_____
_____
_____
_____
_____
_____
_____
_____

Date:	Name of Roller Coaster:	Track Type: ☐ Steel ☐ Wood
Weather:	Name of Park/Location:	Type of Coaster:
Year Opened:	Height:_____ Length:_____ Top Speed:_____	Designer of Coaster:

My Coaster Experience:

_____
_____
_____
_____
_____
_____
_____
_____
_____
_____
_____

Date:	Name of Roller Coaster:	Track Type: ☐ Steel ☐ Wood
Weather:	Name of Park/Location:	Type of Coaster:
Year Opened:	Height:_____ Length:_____ Top Speed:_____	Designer of Coaster:

My Coaster Experience:

_____
_____
_____
_____
_____
_____
_____
_____
_____
_____

Date:	Name of Roller Coaster:	Track Type: ☐ Steel ☐ Wood
Weather:	Name of Park/Location:	Type of Coaster:
Year Opened:	Height:_____ Length:_____ Top Speed:_____	Designer of Coaster:

My Coaster Experience:

_____
_____
_____
_____
_____
_____
_____
_____
_____
_____
_____

Date:	Name of Roller Coaster:	Track Type: ☐ Steel ☐ Wood
Weather:	Name of Park/Location:	Type of Coaster:
Year Opened:	Height:_____ Length:_____ Top Speed:_____	Designer of Coaster:

My Coaster Experience:

_____
_____
_____
_____
_____
_____
_____
_____
_____
_____

Date:	Name of Roller Coaster:	Track Type: ☐ Steel ☐ Wood
Weather:	Name of Park/Location:	Type of Coaster:
Year Opened:	Height:_____ Length:_____ Top Speed:_____	Designer of Coaster:

My Coaster Experience:

_____
_____
_____
_____
_____
_____
_____
_____
_____
_____
_____
_____

Date:	Name of Roller Coaster:	Track Type: ☐ Steel ☐ Wood
Weather:	Name of Park/Location:	Type of Coaster:
Year Opened:	Height:_____ Length:_____ Top Speed:_____	Designer of Coaster:

My Coaster Experience:

_____
_____
_____
_____
_____
_____
_____
_____
_____
_____

Date:	Name of Roller Coaster:	Track Type: ☐ Steel ☐ Wood
Weather: ☀ ⛅ 🌧 🌨	Name of Park/Location:	Type of Coaster:
Year Opened:	Height:_____ Length:_____ Top Speed:_____	Designer of Coaster:

My Coaster Experience:

_____
_____
_____
_____
_____
_____
_____
_____
_____

Date:	Name of Roller Coaster:	Track Type: ☐ Steel ☐ Wood
Weather: ☼ ⛅ 🌧 🌨	Name of Park/Location:	Type of Coaster:
Year Opened:	Height:_____ Length:_____ Top Speed:_____	Designer of Coaster:

My Coaster Experience:

_____

_____

_____

_____

_____

_____

_____

_____

_____

_____

Date:	Name of Roller Coaster:	Track Type: ☐ Steel ☐ Wood
Weather:	Name of Park/Location:	Type of Coaster:
Year Opened:	Height:_____ Length:_____ Top Speed:_____	Designer of Coaster:

My Coaster Experience:

_____

_____

_____

_____

_____

_____

_____

_____

_____

_____

_____

_____

Date:	Name of Roller Coaster:	Track Type: ☐ Steel ☐ Wood
Weather: ☀ ⛅ 🌧 🌨	Name of Park/Location:	Type of Coaster:
Year Opened:	Height:_____ Length:_____ Top Speed:_____	Designer of Coaster:

My Coaster Experience:

_____
_____
_____
_____
_____
_____
_____
_____
_____
_____
_____

Date:	Name of Roller Coaster:	Track Type: ☐ Steel ☐ Wood
Weather:	Name of Park/Location:	Type of Coaster:
Year Opened:	Height:_____ Length:_____ Top Speed:_____	Designer of Coaster:

My Coaster Experience:

_____
_____
_____
_____
_____
_____
_____
_____
_____
_____

Date:	Name of Roller Coaster:	Track Type: ☐ Steel ☐ Wood
Weather:	Name of Park/Location:	Type of Coaster:
Year Opened:	Height:_____ Length:_____ Top Speed:_____	Designer of Coaster:

My Coaster Experience:

_____
_____
_____
_____
_____
_____
_____
_____
_____
_____

Date:	Name of Roller Coaster:	Track Type: ☐ Steel ☐ Wood
Weather:	Name of Park/Location:	Type of Coaster:
Year Opened:	Height:_____ Length:_____ Top Speed:_____	Designer of Coaster:

My Coaster Experience:

_____
_____
_____
_____
_____
_____
_____
_____
_____

Date:	Name of Roller Coaster:	Track Type: ☐ Steel ☐ Wood
Weather: ☀ ⛅ 🌧 ☁	Name of Park/Location:	Type of Coaster:
Year Opened:	Height:_____ Length:_____ Top Speed:_____	Designer of Coaster:

My Coaster Experience:

_____

_____

_____

_____

_____

_____

_____

_____

_____

_____

Date:	Name of Roller Coaster:	Track Type: ☐ Steel ☐ Wood
Weather:	Name of Park/Location:	Type of Coaster:
Year Opened:	Height:_____ Length:_____ Top Speed:_____	Designer of Coaster:

My Coaster Experience:

_____

_____

_____

_____

_____

_____

_____

_____

_____

_____

Date:	Name of Roller Coaster:	Track Type: ☐ Steel ☐ Wood
Weather:	Name of Park/Location:	Type of Coaster:
Year Opened:	Height:_____ Length:_____ Top Speed:_____	Designer of Coaster:

My Coaster Experience:

_____
_____
_____
_____
_____
_____
_____
_____
_____
_____

Date:	Name of Roller Coaster:	Track Type: ☐ Steel ☐ Wood
Weather:	Name of Park/Location:	Type of Coaster:
Year Opened:	Height:_____ Length:_____ Top Speed:_____	Designer of Coaster:

My Coaster Experience:

_____
_____
_____
_____
_____
_____
_____
_____
_____
_____

Date:	Name of Roller Coaster:	Track Type: ☐ Steel ☐ Wood
Weather:	Name of Park/Location:	Type of Coaster:
Year Opened:	Height:_____ Length:_____ Top Speed:_____	Designer of Coaster:

My Coaster Experience:

_____
_____
_____
_____
_____
_____
_____
_____
_____
_____
_____

Date:	Name of Roller Coaster:	Track Type: ☐ Steel ☐ Wood
Weather:	Name of Park/Location:	Type of Coaster:
Year Opened:	Height:_____ Length:_____ Top Speed:_____	Designer of Coaster:

My Coaster Experience:

_____
_____
_____
_____
_____
_____
_____
_____
_____
_____

Date:	Name of Roller Coaster:	Track Type: ☐ Steel ☐ Wood
Weather:	Name of Park/Location:	Type of Coaster:
Year Opened:	Height:_____ Length:_____ Top Speed:_____	Designer of Coaster:

My Coaster Experience:

_____
_____
_____
_____
_____
_____
_____
_____
_____
_____

Date:	Name of Roller Coaster:	Track Type: ☐ Steel ☐ Wood
Weather:	Name of Park/Location:	Type of Coaster:
Year Opened:	Height:_____ Length:_____ Top Speed:_____	Designer of Coaster:

My Coaster Experience:

_____
_____
_____
_____
_____
_____
_____
_____
_____
_____
_____

Date:	Name of Roller Coaster:	Track Type: ☐ Steel ☐ Wood
Weather:	Name of Park/Location:	Type of Coaster:
Year Opened:	Height:_____ Length:_____ Top Speed:_____	Designer of Coaster:

My Coaster Experience:

_____
_____
_____
_____
_____
_____
_____
_____
_____
_____

Date:	Name of Roller Coaster:	Track Type: ☐ Steel ☐ Wood
Weather: ☼ ⛅ 🌧 🌨	Name of Park/Location:	Type of Coaster:
Year Opened:	Height:_____ Length:_____ Top Speed:_____	Designer of Coaster:

My Coaster Experience:

_____

_____

_____

_____

_____

_____

_____

_____

_____

Date:	Name of Roller Coaster:	Track Type: ☐ Steel ☐ Wood
Weather: ☀ ⛅ 🌧 🌨	Name of Park/Location:	Type of Coaster:
Year Opened:	Height:_____ Length:_____ Top Speed:_____	Designer of Coaster:

My Coaster Experience:

_____

_____

_____

_____

_____

_____

_____

_____

_____

_____

Date:	Name of Roller Coaster:	Track Type: ☐ Steel ☐ Wood
Weather: ☀ ⛅ 🌧 🌨	Name of Park/Location:	Type of Coaster:
Year Opened:	Height:_____ Length:_____ Top Speed:_____	Designer of Coaster:

My Coaster Experience:

_____

_____

_____

_____

_____

_____

_____

_____

_____

_____

Date:	Name of Roller Coaster:	Track Type: ☐ Steel ☐ Wood
Weather:	Name of Park/Location:	Type of Coaster:
Year Opened:	Height:_____ Length:_____ Top Speed:_____	Designer of Coaster:

My Coaster Experience:

_____

_____

_____

_____

_____

_____

_____

_____

_____

_____

Date:	Name of Roller Coaster:	Track Type: ☐ Steel ☐ Wood
Weather:	Name of Park/Location:	Type of Coaster:
Year Opened:	Height:_____ Length:_____ Top Speed:_____	Designer of Coaster:

My Coaster Experience:

_____
_____
_____
_____
_____
_____
_____
_____
_____
_____
_____

Date:	Name of Roller Coaster:	Track Type: ☐ Steel ☐ Wood
Weather:	Name of Park/Location:	Type of Coaster:
Year Opened:	Height:_____ Length:_____ Top Speed:_____	Designer of Coaster:

My Coaster Experience:

_____
_____
_____
_____
_____
_____
_____
_____
_____
_____

Date:	Name of Roller Coaster:	Track Type: ☐ Steel ☐ Wood
Weather:	Name of Park/Location:	Type of Coaster:
Year Opened:	Height:_____ Length:_____ Top Speed:_____	Designer of Coaster:

My Coaster Experience:

_____
_____
_____
_____
_____
_____
_____
_____
_____
_____

Date:	Name of Roller Coaster:	Track Type: ☐ Steel ☐ Wood
Weather:	Name of Park/Location:	Type of Coaster:
Year Opened:	Height:_____ Length:_____ Top Speed:_____	Designer of Coaster:

My Coaster Experience:

_____

_____

_____

_____

_____

_____

_____

_____

_____

_____

Date:	Name of Roller Coaster:	Track Type: ☐ Steel ☐ Wood
Weather:	Name of Park/Location:	Type of Coaster:
Year Opened:	Height:_____ Length:_____ Top Speed:_____	Designer of Coaster:

My Coaster Experience:

_____

_____

_____

_____

_____

_____

_____

_____

_____

_____

_____

Date:	Name of Roller Coaster:	Track Type: ☐ Steel ☐ Wood
Weather:	Name of Park/Location:	Type of Coaster:
Year Opened:	Height:_____ Length:_____ Top Speed:_____	Designer of Coaster:

My Coaster Experience:

_____
_____
_____
_____
_____
_____
_____
_____
_____
_____
_____

Date:	Name of Roller Coaster:	Track Type: ☐ Steel ☐ Wood
Weather: ☀ ⛅ 🌧 🌨	Name of Park/Location:	Type of Coaster:
Year Opened:	Height:_____ Length:_____ Top Speed:_____	Designer of Coaster:

My Coaster Experience:

_____

_____

_____

_____

_____

_____

_____

_____

_____

_____

Date:	Name of Roller Coaster:	Track Type: ☐ Steel ☐ Wood
Weather:	Name of Park/Location:	Type of Coaster:
Year Opened:	Height:_____ Length:_____ Top Speed:_____	Designer of Coaster:

My Coaster Experience:

_____
_____
_____
_____
_____
_____
_____
_____
_____
_____

Date:	Name of Roller Coaster:	Track Type: ☐ Steel ☐ Wood
Weather:	Name of Park/Location:	Type of Coaster:
Year Opened:	Height:_____ Length:_____ Top Speed:_____	Designer of Coaster:

My Coaster Experience:

_____

_____

_____

_____

_____

_____

_____

_____

_____

_____

Date:	Name of Roller Coaster:	Track Type: ☐ Steel ☐ Wood
Weather:	Name of Park/Location:	Type of Coaster:
Year Opened:	Height:_____ Length:_____ Top Speed:_____	Designer of Coaster:

My Coaster Experience:

_____

_____

_____

_____

_____

_____

_____

_____

_____

Date:	Name of Roller Coaster:	Track Type: ☐ Steel ☐ Wood
Weather:	Name of Park/Location:	Type of Coaster:
Year Opened:	Height:_____ Length:_____ Top Speed:_____	Designer of Coaster:

My Coaster Experience:

_____
_____
_____
_____
_____
_____
_____
_____
_____
_____

Date:	Name of Roller Coaster:	Track Type: ☐ Steel ☐ Wood
Weather:	Name of Park/Location:	Type of Coaster:
Year Opened:	Height:_____ Length:_____ Top Speed:_____	Designer of Coaster:

My Coaster Experience:

_____
_____
_____
_____
_____
_____
_____
_____
_____
_____
_____
_____

Date:	Name of Roller Coaster:	Track Type: ☐ Steel ☐ Wood
Weather:	Name of Park/Location:	Type of Coaster:
Year Opened:	Height:_____ Length:_____ Top Speed:_____	Designer of Coaster:

My Coaster Experience:

_____

_____

_____

_____

_____

_____

_____

_____

_____

_____

Date:	Name of Roller Coaster:	Track Type: ☐ Steel ☐ Wood
Weather:	Name of Park/Location:	Type of Coaster:
Year Opened:	Height:_____ Length:_____ Top Speed:_____	Designer of Coaster:

My Coaster Experience:

_____
_____
_____
_____
_____
_____
_____
_____
_____
_____

Date:	Name of Roller Coaster:	Track Type: ☐ Steel ☐ Wood
Weather:	Name of Park/Location:	Type of Coaster:
Year Opened:	Height:_____ Length:_____ Top Speed:_____	Designer of Coaster:

My Coaster Experience:

_____
_____
_____
_____
_____
_____
_____
_____
_____
_____
_____

If you enjoyed this journal, we have many more styles and types to choose from. Visit our website for a complete list of journals.

www.wanderingwalksofwonder.com

National Parks Journal

Bucket List Journal

Kid's Travel Journal

Lighthouse Exploration Journal

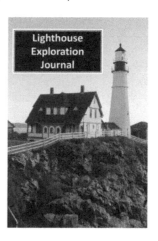

Made in the USA
Middletown, DE
27 November 2018